Bluetooth Tutorial
Design, Protocol and Specifications for BLE - Bluetooth Low Energy 4.0 and Bluetooth 5

Gordon Colbach

gordon.colbach@cloudversity.com

ISBN-13: 9781073331680

REVISION 2

This book is updated regularly and will expand and elaborate on the topic over time. The updates are tracked through a revision number noted above. Updates log can be found in the pages ahead.

If you have already bought an ebook or hard copy then we would be happy to provide you the free ebook of the latest version. Please send an email to the author at gordon.colbach@cloudversity.com to claim your free copy.

CONTENTS

UPDATES

If you have any feedback regarding this book, any errata that you wish to report or updates that you wish to see please shoot out an email to gordon.colbach@cloudversity.com .

As a token of appreciation we will send out an Amazon gift card for every suggestion that we receive.

Update Log

1. 16 Jun 2019 - Launch

2. 24 Sep 2019 - Illustrations added. Grammar fixes.

1. INTRODUCTION

A wireless network is a flexible data communications system, which uses wireless media such as radio frequency technology to transmit and receive data over the air, minimizing the need for wired connections. Wireless networks are used to augment rather than replace wired networks and are most commonly used to provide last few stages of connectivity between a mobile user and a wired network.

Wireless networks use electromagnetic waves to communicate information from one point to another without relying on any physical connection. Radio waves are often referred to as radio carriers because they simply perform the function of delivering energy to a remote receiver. The data being transmitted is superimposed on the radio carrier so that it can be accurately extracted at the receiving end. Once data is superimposed (modulated) onto the radio carrier, the radio signal occupies more than a single frequency, since the frequency or bit rate of the modulating information adds to the carrier.

Multiple radio carriers can exist in the same space at the same time without interfering with each other if the radio waves are transmitted on different radio frequencies. To extract data, a radio receiver tunes in one radio frequency while rejecting all other frequencies. The modulated signal thus received is then demodulated and the data is extracted from the signal.

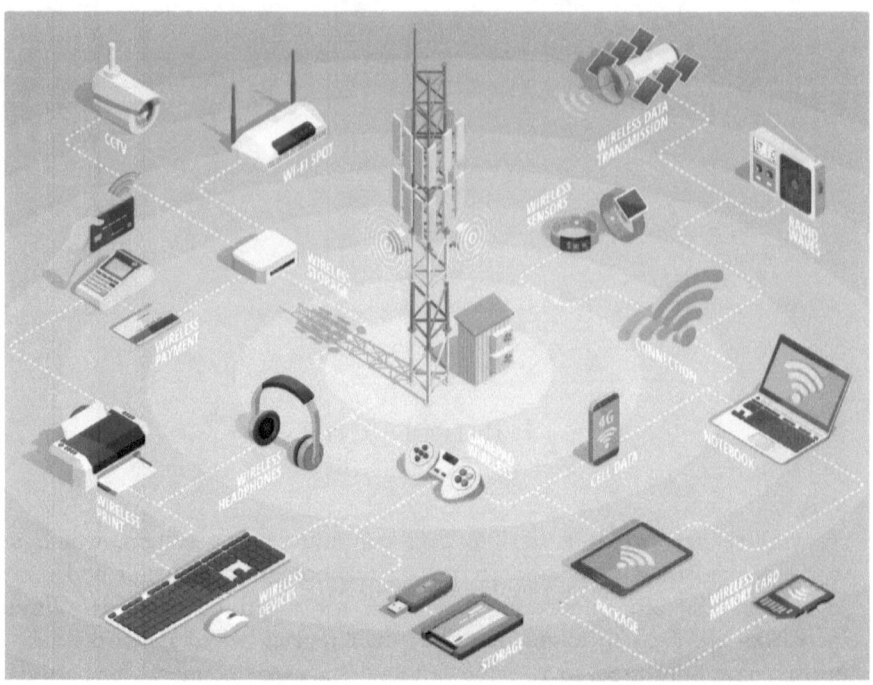

Figure: Wireless Technology

Wireless networks offer the following productivity, convenience, and cost advantages over traditional wired networks:

- **Mobility**: provide mobile users with access to real-time information so that they can roam around in the network without getting disconnected from the network. This mobility supports productivity and service opportunities not possible with wired networks.

- **Installation speed and simplicity**: installing a wireless system can be fast and easy and can eliminate the need to pull cable through walls and ceilings.

- **Reach of the network**: the network can be extended to places which can not be wired

- **More Flexibility**: wireless networks offer more flexibility and adapt easily to changes in the configuration of the network.

- **Reduced cost of ownership**: while the initial investment required for wireless network hardware can be higher than the cost of wired network hardware, overall installation expenses and life- cycle costs can be significantly lower in dynamic environments.

- **Scalability**: wireless systems can be configured in a variety of topologies to meet the needs of specific applications and installations. Configurations can be easily changed and range from peer-to-peer networks suitable for a small number of users to larger infrastructure networks that enable roaming over a broad area.

gordon.colbach@cloudversity.com

2. WIRELESS USAGE SCENARIOS

There are three primary usage scenarios for wireless connectivity [1]:

1. Wireless Personal Area Networking (WPAN)
2. Wireless Local Area Networking (WLAN)
3. Wireless Wide Area Networking (WWAN)

WPAN describes an application of wireless technology that is intended to address usage scenarios that are inherently personal in nature. The emphasis is on instant connectivity between devices that manage personal data or which facilitate data sharing between small groups of individuals.

An example might be synchronizing data between a PDA and a desktop computer. Or another example might be spontaneous sharing of a document between two or more individuals. The nature of these types of data sharing scenarios is that they are ad hoc and often spontaneous. Wireless communication adds value for these types of usage models by reducing complexity (i.e. eliminates the need for cables).

---

[1] "Bluetooth wireless technology basics - HP."
http://www.hp.com/ctg/Manual/c00186949.pdf. Accessed 6 Nov. 2017.

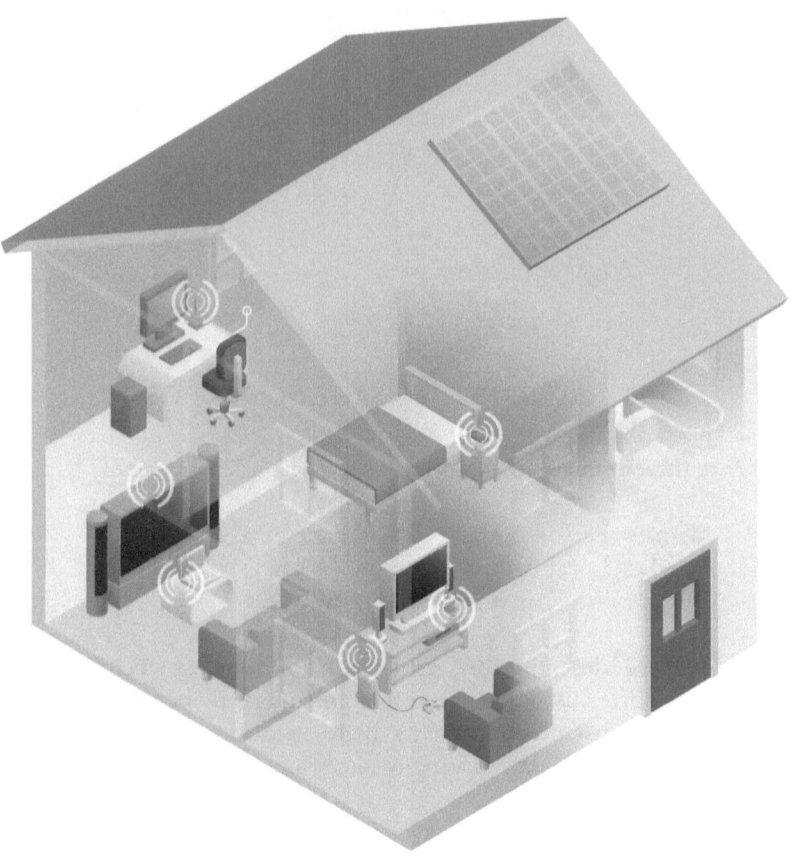

Figure: A home network uses both WLAN and WPAN technologies.

WLAN on the other is more focused on organizational connectivity not unlike wire based LAN connections. The intent of WLAN technologies is to provide members of workgroups access to corporate network resources be it shared data, shared applications or e-mail but do so in a way that does not inhibit a user's mobility. The emphasis is on a permanence of the wireless connection within a defined region like an office building or campus. This implies that there are wireless access points that define a finite region of coverage.

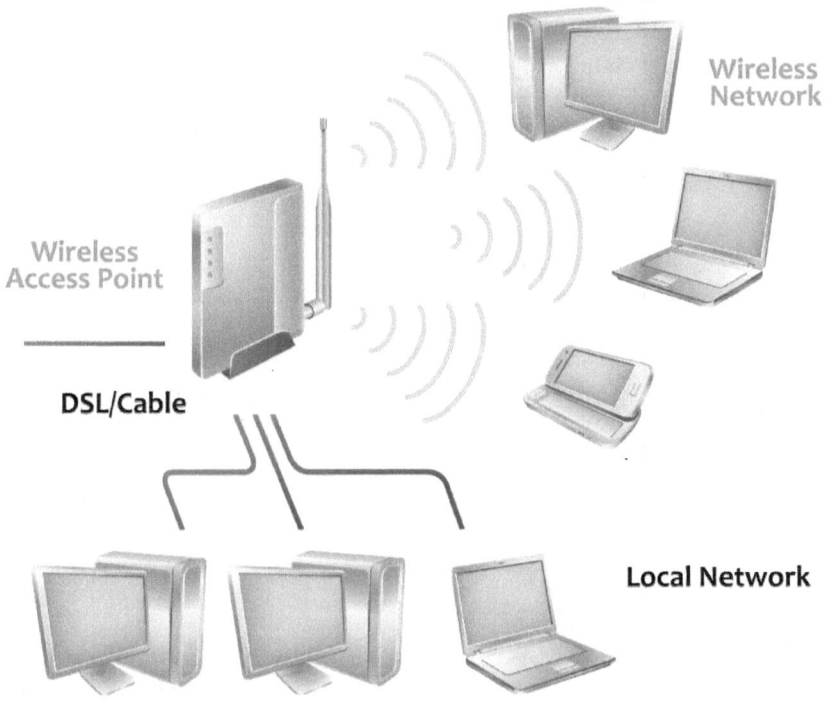

Figure: Wireless Local Area Networks are often extensions of Wired Local Networks

Whereas WLAN addresses connectivity within a defined region, WWAN addresses the need to stay connected while traveling outside this boundary. Today, cellular technologies enable wireless computer connectivity either via a cable to a cellular telephone or through PC Card cellular modems. The need being addressed by WWAN is the need to stay in touch with business critical communications while traveling.

The following table summarizes each wireless connectivity usage scenario by a wireless technology.

Table 1 - Wireless Usage Scenarios by Technology

Wireless Standard	Application Category	Usage Scenario
Bluetooth	WPAN Wireless Personal Area Networking	- I want to instantly connect my notebook computer to another Bluetooth enabled notebook to transfer a file. · I want to work collaboratively on a document ,where meeting participants use notebooks that are wirelessly connected via Bluetooth. · Using a Bluetooth enabled, wireless headset, I want to listen to a CD playing on my notebook computer while it is in my briefcase. · I often travel to a remote site and want to walk up to a shared printer, connect and print a document without having to physically connect using a standard printer cable. · I want to connect to the Internet via a cellular phone without having to take my telephone out of my briefcase
WiFi	WLAN Wireless Local Area Networking	· I want to always be connected to my corporate LAN while moving about in my office building or campus. · Usage demands that I have access to corporate network data at performance levels equivalent to a wire based LAN connection.
Cellular Technology (GSM)	WWAN Wireless Wide Area Networking	· I want access to email and web resources while traveling away from the home office.

Bluetooth and 802.11 are emerging as the preferred technology in the commercial space for WPAN and WLAN respectively. Higher throughput, longer range and other characteristics make 802.11 better suited for WLAN than Bluetooth. The rest of this document gives a basic overview of these two technologies detailing the basic concepts, the principles of operations, and some of the reasons behind some of their features.

3. WHAT IS BLUETOOTH

Bluetooth is the name given to a new technology standard using short-range radio links, intended to replace the cables) connecting portable and/or fixed electronic devices. The standard defines a uniform structure for a wide range of devices to communicate with each other, with minimal user effort.

Its key features are robustness, low complexity, low power and low cost. The technology also offers wireless access to LANs, PSTN, the mobile phone network and the Internet for a host of home appliances and portable handheld interfaces.

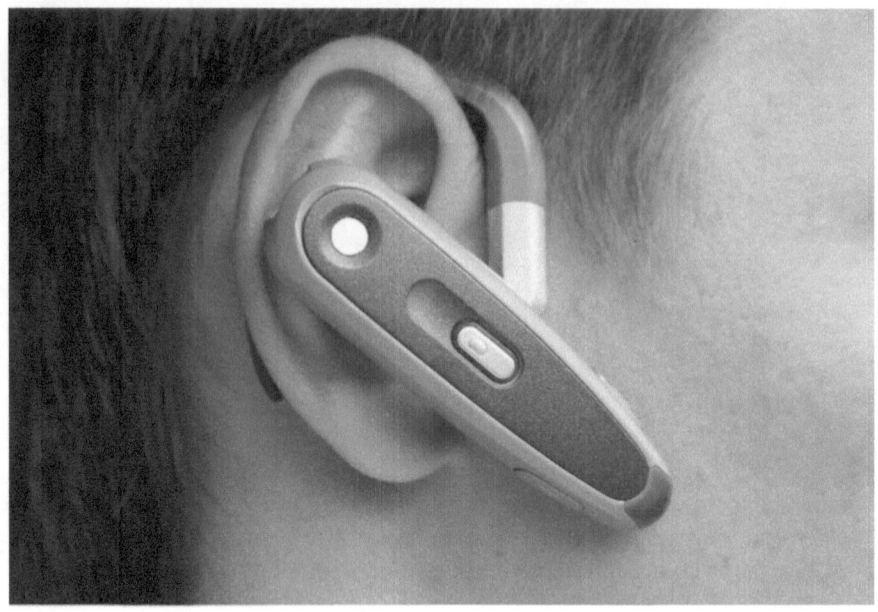

Figure: Bluetooth Headsets - were some of the earliest bluetooth devices to gain consumer traction.

Figure: Bluetooth Speakers are now ubiquitous.

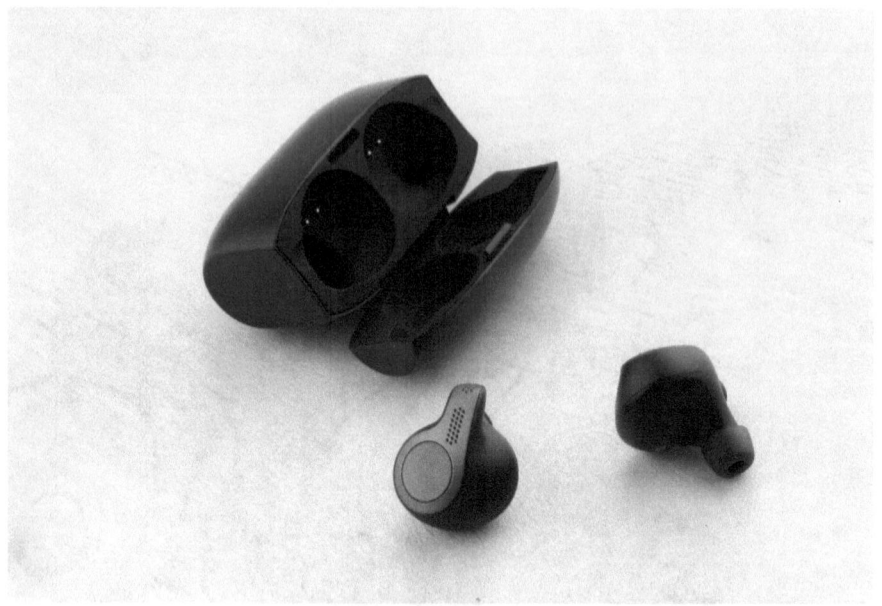

Figure: Bluetooth Earbud Speakers - Continued miniaturization of Bluetooth and battery technology has allowed Earbud shaped speakers.

4. MOTIVATIONS FOR BLUETOOTH

The immediate need for Bluetooth came from the desire to connect peripherals and devices without cables. The available technology-IrDA OBEX (Infrared Data Association Object Exchange Protocol) is based in infrared links that are limited to line of sight connections.

Bluetooth is further fueled by the demand for mobile and wireless access to LANs, Internet over mobile and other existing networks, where the backbone is wired but the interface is free to move. This not only makes the network easier to use but also extends its reach.

The advantages and rapid proliferation of LANs suggest that setting up personal area networks, that is, connections among devices in the proximity of the user, will have many beneficial uses. Bluetooth could also be used in home networking applications. With increasing numbers of homes having multiple PCs, the need for networks that are simple to install and maintain, is growing.

There is also the commercial need to provide "information push" capabilities, which is important for handheld and other such mobile devices and this has been partially incorporated in Bluetooth. Bluetooth's main strength is its ability to simultaneously handle both data and voice transmissions, allowing such innovative solutions as a mobile hands-free headset for voice calls, print to fax capability, and automatically synchronizing

PDA, laptop, and cell phone address book applications.

These uses suggest that a technology like Bluetooth is extremely useful and will have a significant effect on the way information is accessed and used.

5. BLUETOOTH CHARACTERISTICS

Bluetooth radios operate in the unlicensed ISM band at 2.4 Gigahertz using 79 channels between 2.402 GHz to 2.480 GHz (23 channels in some countries)[2]. The range for Bluetooth communication is 0-30 feet (10 meters) with a power consumption of 0 dBm (1 mW). This distance can be increased to 100 meters by amplifying the power to 20dBm.

The Bluetooth radio system is optimized for mobility. Bluetooth supports two kinds of links: Asynchronous Connectionless (ACL) links for data transmission and Synchronous Connection oriented (SCO) links for audio/voice transmission.

The gross Bluetooth data rate is 1 Mbps while the maximum effective rate on an asymmetric ACL link is 721 Kbps in either direction and 57.6 Kbps in the return direction. A symmetric ACL link allows data rates of 432.6 Kbps. Bluetooth also supports up to three 64Kbps SCO channels per device. These channels are guaranteed bandwidth for transmission.

---

[2] "bluetooth | Bluetooth | Communications Protocols - Scribd." https://vi.scribd.com/document/47715483/bluetooth. Accessed 6 Nov. 2017.

6. TECHNOLOGY COMPARISON

Since Bluetooth operates in the unlicensed ISM band that is also used by other devices such as 802.11 networks, baby monitors, garage door openers, microwave ovens etc, there is a possibility of interference. Bluetooth uses Frequency Hop Spread Spectrum (FHSS) to avoid any interference.

A Bluetooth channel is divided into time slots each 625 microsecond in length. The devices hop through these time slots making 1600 hops per second. This trades bandwidth efficiency for reliability, integrity and security.

7. BLUETOOTH ARCHITECTURE

Bluetooth communication occurs between a master radio and a slave radio. Bluetooth radios are symmetric in that the same device may operate as a master and slave. Each radio has a 48-bit unique device address (BD_ADDR) that is fixed.

Two or more radio devices together form ad-hoc networks called piconets. All units within a piconet share the same channel. Each piconet has one master device and one or more slaves.

There may be up to seven active slaves at a time within a piconet. Thus, each active device within a piconet is identifiable by a 3-bit active device address. Inactive slaves in unconnected modes may continue to reside within the piconet.

A master is the only one that may initiate a Bluetooth communication link. However, once a link is established, the slave may request a master/slave switch to become the master. Slaves are not allowed to talk to each other directly. All communication occurs within the slave and the master.

Slaves within a piconet must also synchronize their internal clocks and frequency hops with that of the master. Each piconet uses a different frequency hopping sequence. Radio devices used Time Division Multiplexing (TDM). A master device in a piconet transmits on even numbered slots and the slaves may transmit on odd numbered slots.

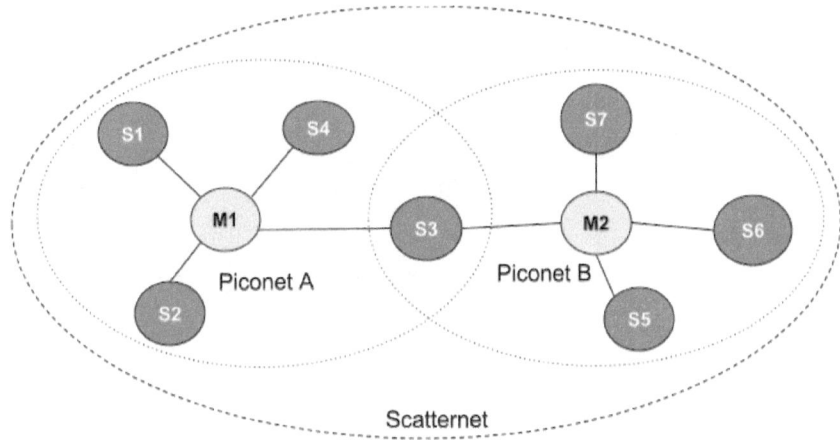

Figure 1: Bluetooth Scatternets and Piconets

Multiple piconets with overlapping coverage areas form a scatternet. Each piconet may have only one master, but slaves may participate in different piconets on a time-division multiplex basis. A device may be a master in one piconet and a slave in another or a slave in more than one piconet.

8. BLUETOOTH PROTOCOL STACK

The Bluetooth Special Interest Group (SIG) [3] has developed the Bluetooth Protocol Stack. These specifications allow for developing interactive services and applications over interoperable radio modules and data communication protocols. Given below is an overview of the protocols in the specification.

The main objective of these specifications is to set down the protocols that must be followed by companies when manufacturing and developing both software and hardware to interoperate with each other. To achieve this interoperability, matching applications (e.g., corresponding client and server application) in remote devices must run over identical protocol stacks.

Different applications may run over different protocol stacks however they will all have one imperative factor that will allow them to be interoperable and that will be the use of a common Bluetooth data link and physical layer.

The complete Bluetooth protocol stack is shown in Figure 2. It may seem that an application must use all protocols shown however not all applications will make use of all the protocols shown. Instead, applications run over one or more vertical slices from this protocol stack.

The main principle in mind when developing the Bluetooth Protocol

---

[3] "Bluetooth SIG." https://www.bluetooth.com/. Accessed 7 Nov. 2017.

Architecture has been the maximization and the re-use of existing protocols for different purposes at the higher layers. The one main advantage is that existing (legacy) applications can be adapted to work with the Bluetooth Technology.

The Bluetooth Protocol Architecture also allows for the use of commonly used application protocols on top of the Bluetooth-Specific protocols. In simpler terms, this permits new applications to take full advantage of the capabilities of the Bluetooth technology and for many applications that are already developed by vendors; they can take immediate advantage of hardware and software systems, which are also compliant with the Specification.

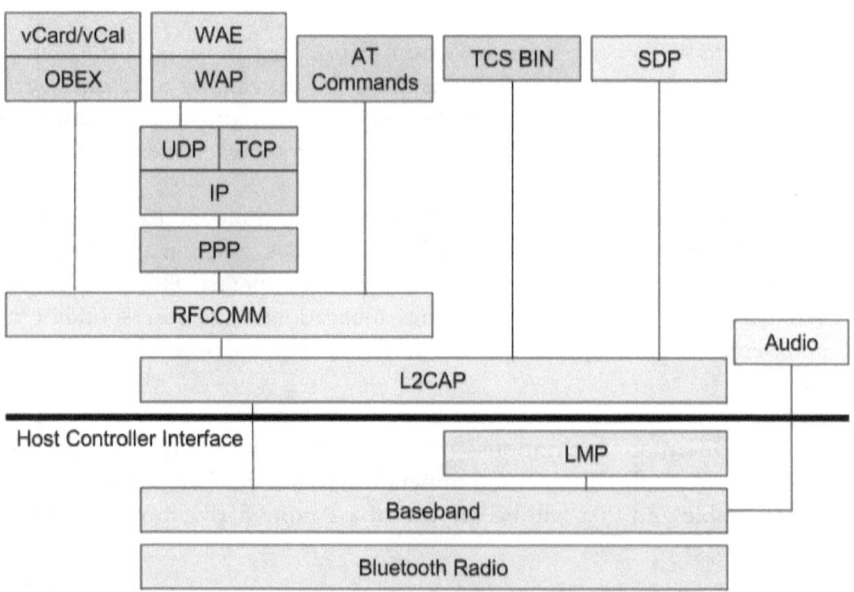

Figure 2: The Bluetooth Protocol Stack Model

Table 2: The protocols and layers in the Bluetooth protocol stack

Protocol Layer	Protocols in the stack [4]
Bluetooth Core Protocols	Baseband , LMP, L2CAP, SDP
Cable Replacement Protocol	RFCOMM
Telephony Control Protocol	TCS Binary, AT-commands, Headset, FAX, Dial-Up
Adopted Protocols	PPP [5], UDP/TCP/IP [6], OBEX, WAP, VCard [7], vCalendar [8], IrMC [9], WAE [10]

In addition to the above protocol layers, the Specification also defines a Host Controller Interface (HCI). This provides a command interface to the baseband controller, link manager, and access to hardware status and control

---

[4] "Specifications | Bluetooth Technology Website - Bluetooth SIG." https://www.bluetooth.com/specifications. Accessed 6 Nov. 2017.
[5] "Request for Comments (RFC) Pages - IETF." https://www.ietf.org/rfc.html. Accessed 6 Nov. 2017.
[6] "Request for Comments (RFC) Pages - IETF." https://www.ietf.org/rfc.html. Accessed 6 Nov. 2017.
[7] "RFC 6350 - vCard Format Specification - IETF Tools." https://tools.ietf.org/html/rfc6350. Accessed 6 Nov. 2017.
[8] "Internet Mail Consortium." https://www.imc.org/. Accessed 6 Nov. 2017.
[9] "IrMC: Infrared Solutions for Mobile Communications." http://www.electroscheme.ru/datasheet/IrDA/irmc_solutions.pdf. Accessed 6 Nov. 2017.
[10] "WAP Forum Specifications." http://www.wapforum.org/what/technical.htm. Accessed 6 Nov. 2017.

registers.

The Bluetooth Core protocols (plus the Bluetooth radio) are required by most of Bluetooth devices while the rest of the protocols are used only as needed. The combination of The Cable Replacement layer, the Telephony Control layer and the adopted protocol layer form the application-oriented protocols which enable applications to run over the Bluetooth Core protocols table

9. Bluetooth Core Protocols

9.1. Baseband [11]

The Baseband and Link Control layer enables the physical RF link between Bluetooth forming a piconet. As the Bluetooth RF system is a Frequency-Hopping-Spread-Spectrum system in simpler terms packets are transmitted in defined time slots on defined frequencies, this synchronizes the transmission hopping frequency and clock of different Bluetooth devices.

It provides two different kinds of physical links with their corresponding baseband packets, Synchronous Connection-Oriented and Asynchronous Connectionless which can be transmitted in a multiplexing manner on the same RF link. Asynchronous Connectionless (ACL) packets are used for the transmission of data only while Synchronous Connection-Oriented can contain audio only or a combination of audio and data.

---

[11] "Specifications | Bluetooth Technology Website."
https://www.bluetooth.com/specifications. Accessed 6 Nov. 2017.

All audio and data packets can be provided with different levels of FEC or CRC error correction and can be encrypted. Furthermore, the different data types, including link management and control messages, are each allocated a special channel.

Audio data can be transferred between one or more Bluetooth devices, making various usage models possible and audio data in SCO packets is routed directly to and from Baseband and it does not go through L2CAP. Audio model is relatively simple within Bluetooth; any two Bluetooth devices can send and receive audio data between each other just by opening an audio link.

9.2. Link Manager Protocol

The link manager protocol is responsible for link set-up between Bluetooth devices. This includes setting up of security functions like authentication and encryption by generating, exchanging and checking of link and encryption keys and the control and negotiation of baseband packet sizes. Furthermore it controls the power modes and duty cycles of the Bluetooth radio device, and the connection states of a Bluetooth unit in a piconet.

9.3. Logical Link Control and Adaptation Protocol

The Bluetooth logical link control and adaptation protocol (L2CAP) adapts upper layer protocols over the baseband. It can be thought to work in parallel with LMP in difference that L2CAP provides services to the upper layer when the payload data is never sent at LMP messages.

L2CAP provides connection-oriented and connectionless data services to the upper layer protocols with protocol multiplexing capability, segmentation and reassembly operation, and group abstractions. L2CAP permits higher-level protocols and applications to transmit and receive L2CAP data packets up to 64 kilobytes in length.

Although the Baseband protocol provides the SCO and ACL link types,L2CAP is defined only for ACL links and no support for SCO links is specified in Bluetooth Specification 1.0.

9.4. Service Discovery Protocol

Discovery services are crucial part of the Bluetooth framework. These services provide the basis for all the usage models. Using SDP, device information, services and the characteristics of the services can be queried and after that, a connection between two or more Bluetooth devices can be established. SDP is defined in the Service Discovery Protocol specification.

9.5. The Cable Replacement Protocol

9.5.1 RFCOMM [12]

RFCOMM is a serial line emulation protocol and is based on ETSI 07.10 (European Telecommunications Standardization Institute) specification. This "cable replacement" protocol emulates RS-232 control and data signals over Bluetooth baseband, providing both transport capabilities for upper level services (e.g. OBEX) that use serial line as transport mechanism.

---

[12] "Core Specifications | Bluetooth Technology Website." https://www.bluetooth.com/specifications/bluetooth-core-specification. Accessed 6 Nov. 2017.

9.6. Telephony Control Protocol

Telephony Control protocol - Binary (TCS Binary or TCS BIN), a bit oriented protocol, defines the call control signaling for the establishment of speech and data calls between Bluetooth devices. In addition, it defines mobility management procedures for handling groups of Bluetooth TCS devices. TCS Binary is specified in the Bluetooth Telephony Control protocol Specification Binary, which is based on the ITU-T Recommendation Q.931[13], applying the symmetrical provisions as stated in Annex D of Q.931.

---

[13] "Traditional Profile Specifications | Bluetooth Technology Website." https://www.bluetooth.com/specifications/profiles-overview. Accessed 6 Nov. 2017.

10. BLUETOOTH ADOPTED PROTOCOLS

10.1. PPP

In Bluetooth technologies PPP is designed to run over RFCOMM to accomplish point to point connection. PPP is the IETF Point-to-Point Protocol and PPP-Networking is the means of taking IP packets to/from the PPP layer and placing them onto the LAN. Usage of PPP over Bluetooth is described in [14].

---

[14] "Traditional Profile Specifications | Bluetooth Technology Website." https://www.bluetooth.com/specifications/profiles-overview. Accessed 6 Nov. 2017.

10.2. TCP/UDP/IP

These protocol standards are already defined by the Internet Engineering Task Force and used commonly in communication across the Internet. The TCP/IP stacks are used in numerous devices including printers, handheld computers and mobile handsets the use of the TCP/IP protocol in the Bluetooth Specification

Protocol for the implementation in Bluetooth devices allows for communication with any other device connected to the Internet. The Bluetooth device should be a Bluetooth cellular handset or a data access point for example is then used as a bridge to the Internet. TCP/IP/PPP is used for the all Internet Bridge usage scenarios in Bluetooth 1.0 and for OBEX in future versions [15]. UDP/IP/PPP is also available as transport for WAP [16].

---

[15] "Protocol Specifications | Bluetooth Technology Website."
https://www.bluetooth.com/specifications/protocol-specifications. Accessed 6 Nov. 2017.
[16] "Core Specifications | Bluetooth Technology Website."
https://www.bluetooth.com/specifications/bluetooth-core-specification.
Accessed 6 Nov. 2017.

10.3. OBEX Protocol

IrOBEX [17] (shortly OBEX) is a session protocol developed by the Infrared Data Association (IrDA) to exchange objects in a simple and spontaneous manner. OBEX, which provides the same basic functionality as HTTP but in a much lighter fashion, uses a client-server model and is independent of the transport mechanism and transport API, provided it realizes a reliable transport base.

Along with the protocol itself, the "grammar" for OBEX conversations between devices, OBEX also provides a model for representing objects and operations. In addition, the OBEX protocol defines a folder-listing object, which is used to browse the contents of folders on remote device. In the first phase, RFCOMM is used as sole transport layer for OBEX. Future implementations are likely to support also TCP/IP as a transport.

[17] "Infrared Data Communications with IrDA."
http://kurser.iha.dk/eit/dtm3/IrDA/intro_prot.pdf. Accessed 6 Nov. 2017.

10.4. Content Formats

vCard [18] and vCalendar [19] are open specifications developed by the versit consortium and now controlled by the Internet Mail Consortium. These specifications define the format of an electronic business card and personal calendar entries and scheduling information, respectively.

vCard and vCalendar do not define any transport mechanism but only the format under which data is transported. By adopting the vCard and vCalendar, the SIG will help further promote the exchange of personal information under these well defined and supported formats. The vCard and vCalendar specifications are available from the Internet Mail Consortium and are being further developed by the Internet Engineering Task Force (IETF).

Other content formats, which are transferred by OBEX in Bluetooth, are vMessage and vNote. These content formats are also open standards and are used to exchange messages and notes. They are defined in the IrMC (Infrared Mobile Communications) specification, which also defines a format for the log files that are needed when synchronizing data between devices.

---

[18] "vCard - Wikipedia." https://en.wikipedia.org/wiki/VCard. Accessed 6 Nov. 2017.

[19] "vCalendar - Just Solve the File Format Problem." 2 Apr. 2017, http://fileformats.archiveteam.org/wiki/VCalendar. Accessed 6 Nov. 2017.

10.5. WAP

The main advantage of using WAP features in Bluetooth technologies is to build application gateways, which will mediate between WAP servers and some other application on the PC. In simpler terms, this will provide functions like remote control and data fetching from PC to handset. The idea behind the use of WAP is to reuse the upper software application developed for the WAP Application Environment.

11. BLUETOOTH USAGE MODELS

In the following text, the highest priority usage models identified by the SIG's marketing group are briefly introduced. Each usage model is accompanied by a Profile. Profiles define the protocols and protocol features supporting a particular usage model. Bluetooth SIG has specified the profiles for these usage models.

In addition to these profiles, there are four general profiles that are widely utilized by these usage model oriented profiles. These are the generic access profile (GAP), the serial port profile, the service discovery application profile (SDAP), and the generic object exchange profile (GOEP). [20]

---

[20] "Bluetooth SIG." https://www.bluetooth.com/. Accessed 6 Nov. 2017.

11.1. File Transfer

The file transfer usage model offers the ability to transfer data objects from one device (e.g., PC, smartphone, or PDA) to another. Object types include, but are not limited to, .xls, .ppt, .wav, .jpg, and .doc files, entire folders or directories or streaming media formats. Also, this usage model offers a possibility to browse the contents of the folders on a remote device.

In Figure 3, the required protocol stack presented for this usage model is presented. The figure does not show the LMP, Baseband, and Radio layers although those are used underneath (See Figure 2).

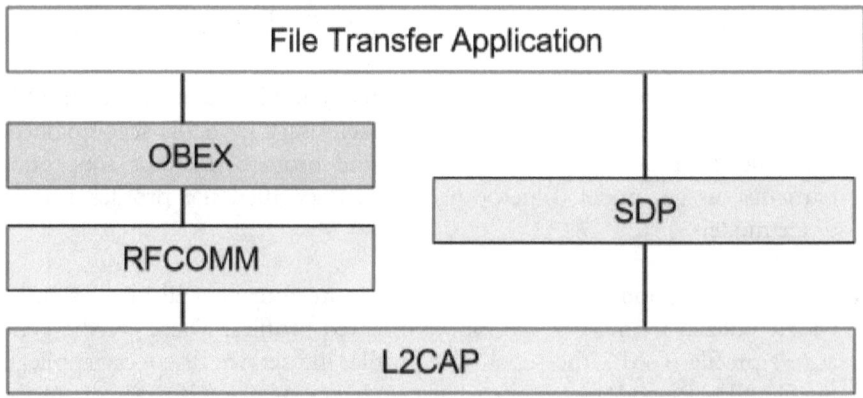

Figure 3: Protocol Stack for File Transfer Applications

11.2. Synchronization

The synchronization usage model provides a device-to-device (phone, PDA, computer, etc.) synchronization of the PIM (personal information management) information, typically phonebook, calendar, message, and note information. Synchronization requires business card, calendar and task information to be transferred and processed by computers, cellular phones and PDAs utilizing a common protocol and format.

The protocol stack for this usage model is presented in Figure 4. In the figure, the synchronization application block represents either an IrMC client or an IrMC server software.

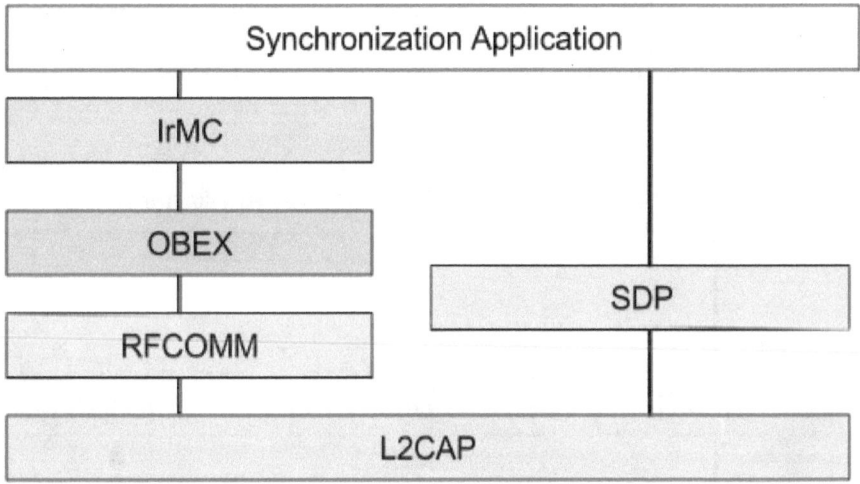

Figure 4: Protocol Stack for Synchronization

11.3. Three-in-One Phone

Telephone handsets built to this profile may connect to three different service providers. First, telephones may act as cordless phones connecting to the public switched telephone network (PSTN) at home or the office and incurring a fixed line charge. This scenario includes making calls via a voice base station, making direct calls between two terminals via the base station and accessing supplementary services provided by an external network.

Second, telephones can connect directly to other telephones for the purpose of acting as a "walkie-talkie" or handset extension. Referred to as the intercom scenario, the connection incurs no additional charge. Third, the telephone may act as a cellular phone connecting to the cellular infrastructure and incurring cellular charges. The cordless and intercom scenarios use the same protocol stack, which is shown in Figure 5. The audio stream is directly connected to the Baseband protocol indicated by the L2CAP bypassing audio arrow.

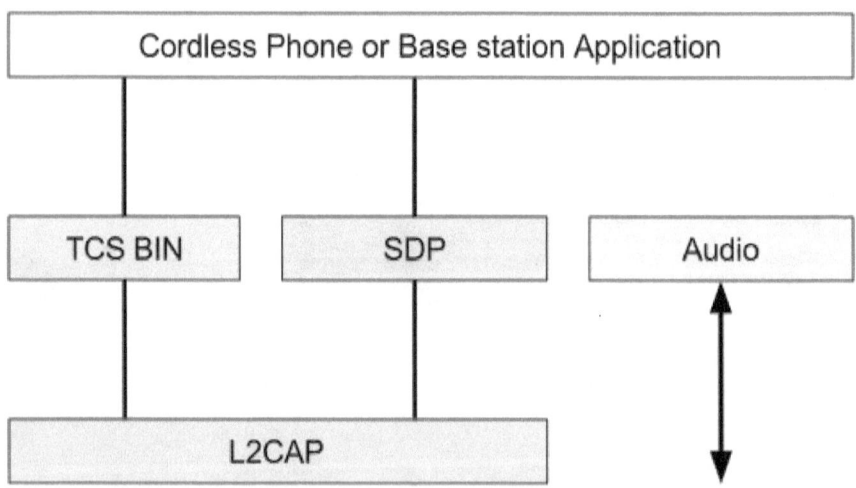

Figure 5: Protocol Stack for Cordless Phone and Intercom Scenarios

11.4. Ultimate Headset

The headset can be wirelessly connected for the purpose of acting as a remote device's audio input and output interface. The headset increases the user's freedom of movement while maintaining call privacy. A common example is a scenario where a headset is used with either a cellular handset, cordless handset, or personal computer for audio input and output.

The protocol stack for this usage model is depicted in Figure 6. The audio stream is directly connected to the Baseband protocol indicated by the L2CAP bypassing audio arrow. The headset must be able to send AT-commands (Attention commands) and receive result codes. This ability allows the headset to answer incoming calls and then terminate them without physically manipulating the telephone handset.

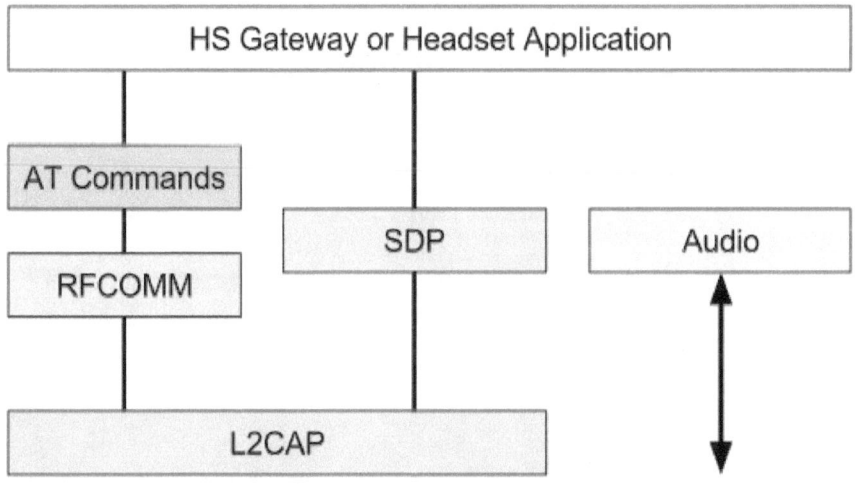

Figure 6: Ultimate Headset Protocol Stack

Figure: Bluetooth Headsets sync with a smartphone to allow for wireless telephony.

12. BLUETOOTH PROTOCOLS SUMMARY

The Bluetooth Protocol Architecture has been developed by the Bluetooth Special Interest Group (SIG) are intended for rapidly developing applications using Bluetooth technology.

The lower layers of the Bluetooth stack are designed to provide a flexible base for further protocol development. RFCOMM protocols are adopted from existing protocols and these protocols and have been only slightly modified for the purpose of Bluetooth.

The upper layer protocols are used without modifications this has been to allow existing applications to be reused to work with the Bluetooth technology and the interoperability is ensured more easily.

13. BLUETOOTH SPECIFICATIONS

Bluetooth Specifications are managed by the Bluetooth Special Interest Group (SIG) which is represents a consortium of around 30,000 companies world wide. This allows for a broader adoption of bluetooth technology and has helped consumers by allowing for a wider range of interoperability amongst Bluetooth enabled products.

The Bluetooth SIG was set up around May 1998 and periodically sets up working groups around future protocol updates and ratifies protocol upgrades periodically. These upgrades are primarily focused around 4 specific areas:

1. Bluetooth Core Specification: This is a major upgrade of the core specification and sees a release every 2-3 years.

2. Core Specification Addendum (CSA): Any additions to a core specification go here and can happen monthly following a core specification launch.

3. Core Specification Supplements (CSS): Any updates which are not ready to be launched along with a core specification launch are optionally launched later as supplements.

4. Specification Errata: Includes fixes to any errors which might have crept into an earlier core release.

13.1. Bluetooth 1.0 and 1.0B

The first version of the Bluetooth specification were ratified around early 2000. The first version of the Bluetooth saw very little adoption interest because it was riddled with problems, even by the time 1.0B was ratified. [21]

Even though the launch of 1.0/1.0B was a significant milestone in the evolution of Bluetooth, it was only post Bluetooth 1.1 that the adoption story really start.

13.2. Bluetooth 1.1

Bluetooth 1.1 was published in June 2002 as IEEE 802.15.1-2002[22]. The primary purpose of 1.1 was to fix the numerous errata which were reported in 1.0 and 1.0B.

Bluetooth 1.1 also had significant improvements to the Bluetooth security model and updates on service discovery.

---

[21] "Why Bluetooth 1.1? | Why Change at All? | InformIT." 11 May. 2001, http://www.informit.com/articles/article.aspx?p=21323. Accessed 17 Apr. 2018.
[22] "IEEE 802.15.1." http://www.ieee802.org/15/pub/TG1.html. Accessed 17 Apr. 2018.

13.3. Bluetooth 1.2

Bluetooth 1.2 was ratified around mid 2005 and primarily focused on improving transmission speeds (upto 721 kbit/s) over Bluetooth 1.1.[23]

Bluetooth 1.2 also introduced updates to enable faster connection and discovery of newer devices. Specific updates were also introduced to enable high quality audio throughput by allowing for retransmission of corrupted audio data packets.[24]

---

[23] "IEEE Std 802.15.1-2005, Part 15.1: Wireless MAC and PHY ...." 14 Jun. 2005, http://www.sj.ifsc.edu.br/~msobral/RCO2/docs/ieee/802.15.1-2005.pdf. Accessed 17 Apr. 2018.
[24] "Bluetooth SIG announces 1.2 specification - Geek.com." 7 Nov. 2003, https://www.geek.com/blurb/bluetooth-sig-announces-12-specification-553676/. Accessed 17 Apr. 2018.

13.4. Bluetooth 2.0 + EDR

Bluetooth 2.0 was launched in 2004 and allowed for an optional feature called Enhanced Data Rate (EDR) for faster data transfer. [25]

EDR allowed for a theoretical bit rate of 3 Mbit/s which was more than a 300% increase over the 721 kbit/s possible with Bluetooth 1.2. Even though the practical bit rate was around 2.1 Mbit/s after allowing for packet acknowledgements this was a critical jump which allowed Bluetooth to dominate audio streaming over the years.

13.5. Bluetooth 2.1 + EDR

Bluetooth 2.1 + EDR was launched by the SIG in July 2007[26]. The 2.1 included the EDR extension of version 2.0 and added enhanced support for ad hoc pairing of bluetooth devices.

The so called **Secure Simple Pairing (SSP)** option dramatically simplified the pairing experience for Bluetooth enabled devices and also increased security at the same time.

[25] "What is Bluetooth 2.0+EDR? - Definition from WhatIs.com."
http://whatis.techtarget.com/definition/Bluetooth-20EDR. Accessed 17 Apr. 2018.
[26] "Bluetooth 2.1 + EDR unveiled - Engadget." 30 Mar. 2007,
https://www.engadget.com/2007/03/30/bluetooth-2-1-edr-unveiled/. Accessed 17 Apr. 2018.

13.6. Bluetooth 3.0 + HS

Bluetooth version 3.0 was ratified by the Bluetooth SIG in April 2009. The launch feature for Bluetooth 3.0 was the optional **High Speed (HS)** support.[27]

The **High Speed** improved the theoretical data speed from 3 Mbit/s to upto 24 MBit/s. The caveat was that this did not happen directly over the Bluetooth link itself.

To provide for the high speed option a new feature called **Alternate MAC/PHY (AMP)** was introduced. The AMP is an optional feature which allowed for data transfer over an alternate 802.11 MAC layer after the initial Bluetooth link was established.

[27] "New features and advantages of Bluetooth 3.0+HS - The Windows Club." 24 Feb. 2011, http://www.thewindowsclub.com/new-features-and-advantages-of-bluetooth-3-0hs. Accessed 17 Apr. 2018.

13.7. Bluetooth 4.0 + LE

Bluetooth Version 4.0, also known as **Bluetooth Smart** was ratified by the SIG around June 2010. [28]

The big addition to Bluetooth was the optional **Low Energy (LE)** support. Bluetooth Low Energy introduced an entirely new protocol stack based on a technology earlier known as Wibree [29].

Bluetooth Low Energy dramatically simplified the discovery and pairing of simple links throughout the Bluetooth protocol stack and was aimed at reducing the radio power usage throughout. More importantly this was done without compromising the traditional Bluetooth communication range.

In addition to Bluetooth Low Energy, Bluetooth Smart also introduced the earlier Bluetooth High Speed (HS) and the Classic Bluetooth protocols.

13.8. Bluetooth 4.1

Bluetooth version 4.1 was announced on December 2013[30] and was largely an incremental software update to the 4.0 specification. It did not introduce any new headline features over the 4.0 release.

---

[28] "Bluetooth Low Energy - Wikipedia."
https://en.wikipedia.org/wiki/Bluetooth_Low_Energy. Accessed 17 Apr. 2018.
[29] "What is Wibree (Baby Bluetooth)? - Definition from WhatIs.com."
https://searchmobilecomputing.techtarget.com/definition/Wibree. Accessed 17 Apr. 2018.
[30] "Bluetooth 4.1 introduced with new features, development flexibility ...." 4 Dec. 2013, https://www.androidcentral.com/bluetooth-41-introduced-new-features-flexibility. Accessed 17 Apr. 2018.

13.9. Bluetooth 4.2

As Bluetooth gained traction and rapidly dominated the Wireless Personal Area Network (WPAN) scenario, it was felt that the next wave of Bluetooth growth will come from the rapidly growing applications around **Internet of Things**. [31]

Consequently, Bluetooth 4.2 was released on December 2014 and was the first version of Bluetooth to introduce support for **Internet of Things** (IOT) usage. The IOT support was further reinforced by security and transmission updates to Bluetooth Low Energy.

---

[31] "Bluetooth 4.2 is faster, safer, and lets lightbulbs connect to the internet ...." 3 Dec. 2014, https://www.theverge.com/2014/12/3/7330117/bluetooth-4-2-is-faster-safer-and-lets-lightbulbs-connect-to-the. Accessed 17 Apr. 2018.

13.10. Bluetooth 5

Launched in June 2016, Bluetooth 5[32] furthered the SIG's ambitions to get Bluetooth to play an increasing role in the Internet of Things scenarios. The core upgrades in Bluetooth 5 allowed for increased bandwidth over Bluetooth Low Energy connections.

The increased speeds reached around 2 MBit/s, which was twice the bandwidth supported over Bluetooth 4. However the increased speeds came at the expense of range. Similar options were provided for increased ranges at the expense of speed and higher throughputs by expanding packet lengths.

Bluetooth 5 is the latest Bluetooth specification to go live at the time of this writing. It has gained rapid adoption and Bluetooth 5 support was seen in some of the smartphone flagships launched during 2017. This included the Samsung Galaxy S8 and Apple iPhone flagships launched during late 2017.

---

[32] "Bluetooth 5 - Go Faster. Go Further. | Bluetooth Technology Website." https://www.bluetooth.com/bluetooth-technology/bluetooth5/bluetooth5-paper. Accessed 17 Apr. 2018.

14. CONNECTION ESTABLISHMENT IN BLUETOOTH

This section describes the basic procedures to be followed by two or more Bluetooth devices to start a connection between themselves[33].

Consider the following scenario: A person walks into a hotel lobby and wants to access her email over her Bluetooth enabled device, which could be a laptop or a Personal Digital Assistant. What would she do ?

Depending on the implementation., she would be clicking on a menu or an email application icon. The device would automatically carry out the following steps, (except perhaps for the authentication step if the device has come to the environment for the first time):

1. **Inquiry**: The device on reaching a new environment would automatically initiated an inquiry to find out what access points are within its range. (If not, it'll do so when the email application asks for a link.) This will result in the following events:
   a. All nearby access points respond with their addresses.
   b. The device picks one out the responding devices.

2. **Paging**: The device will invoke a baseband procedure called paging.

---

[33] "Bluetooth: Connect Without Cables: Jennifer Bray, Charles F. Sturman ...." https://www.amazon.com/Bluetooth-Connect-Without-Jennifer-Bray/dp/0130898406. Accessed 6 Nov. 2017.

This results in synchronization of the device with the access point, in terms of its clock offset and phase in the frequency hop, among other required initializations.

3. **Link establishment**: The LMP will now establish a link with the access point. As the application in this case is email, an ACL link will be used. Various setup steps will be carried out as described below.

4. **Service Discovery**: The LMP will use the SDP (Service Discovery Protocol) to discover what services are available from the access point, in particular whether email access or access to the relevant host is possible from this access point or not. Let us assume that the service is available, otherwise, the application cannot proceed further. The information regarding the other services offered at the access point may be presented to the user.

5. **L2CAP channel**: With information obtained from SDP, the device will create an L2CAP channel to the access point. This may be directly used by the application or another protocol like RFCOMM may be run over it.

6. **RFCOMM channel**: Depending on the need of the email application an RFCOMM or other channel (in case of other applications) will be created over the L2CAP channel. This feature allows existing applications developed for serial ports to run without modification over Bluetooth platforms.

7. **Security**: If the access point restricts its access to a particular set of users or otherwise offers secure mode communications to people having some prior registration with it, then at this stage, the access point will send a security request for "pairing". This will be successful if the user knows the correct PIN code to access the service. Note that the PIN is not transmitted over the wireless channel but another key generated from it is used, so that the PIN is difficult to compromise. Encryption will be invoked if secure mode is used.

8. **PPP**: If a PPP link is used over serial modem as in dial up networking, the same application will now be able to run PPP over RFCOMM (which emulates the serial port). This link will allow the user to login to his email account.

9. **Network Protocols**: The network protocols like TCP/IP, IPX , Appletalk can now send and receive data over the link.

In the above procedure, user interaction is required only at the usual login for his email and additionally for the security to be implemented. The remaining steps are automatic.

15. BLUETOOTH SECURITY

Bluetooth has powerful security features with the SAFER+(Secure And Fast Encryption Routine) encryption engine using up to 128 bit keys. At the Link Level, it is possible to authenticate a device. This verifies that a pair of devices share a secret key derived from a Bluetooth passkey, also known as a Personal Identification Number (PIN). The Bluetooth passkey is entered either in a user interface or for devices such as headsets, which do not have a user interface, the manufacturer can build it in.

After authentication, devices can create shared link keys, which can be used to encrypt traffic on a link. The combination of authentication and creating link keys is calling pairing, possibly accompanied by exchange of higher-level security information, and is called bonding.

Authentication may be repeated after pairing, in which case the link key is used as the shared secret key. Three modes of security can be implemented: Mode 1 is not secure, Mode 2 has security imposed at the request of applications and services, and Mode 3 has security imposed when any new connection is established.

16. BLUETOOTH VS. THE WORLD

Bluetooth has emerged as the preferred wireless technology for WPAN. The only other competing technology was Infrared Technology, known as IrDA.

IrDA is the most economical wireless connectivity solution to implement. In spite of an installed base of over 100 million units worldwide, a series of limitations has greatly reduced its potential.

Although operating at a transfer rate of 4 Mbps IrDA requires line-of-sight between appliances which significantly reduces usability, its short operating range of 1 meter is a major limitation that has allowed Bluetooth to replace it.

As the installed base for Bluetooth grows the need for IrDA will likely decrease further.

gordon.colbach@cloudversity.com

17. ZIGBEE

When you hold the TV remote and wish to use it you have to necessarily point your control at the device. This one-way, line-of-sight, short-range communication uses infrared (IR) sensors to enable communication and control and it is possible to operate the TV remotely only with its control unit.

Add other home theatre modules, an air- conditioner and remotely enabled fans and lights to your room, and you become a juggler who has to handle not only these remotes, but also more numbers that will accompany other home appliances you are likely to use.

Some remotes do serve to control more than one device after 'memorizing' access codes, but this interoperability is restricted to LOS, that too only for a set of related equipment, like the different units of a home entertainment system

Now picture a home with entertainment units, security systems including fire alarm, smoke detector and burglar alarm, air-conditioners and kitchen appliances all within whispering distance from each other and imagine a single unit that talks with all the devices, no longer depending on line-of-sight, and traffic no longer being one-way.

This means that the devices and the control unit would all need a common standard to enable intelligible communication. ZigBee is a standard for embedded application software and has been ratified in late 2004 under IEEE 802.15.4 Wireless Networking Standards.

ZigBee is an established set of specifications for wireless personal area networking (WPAN), i.e., digital radio connections between computers and related devices. This kind of network eliminates use of physical data buses like USB and Ethernet cables. The devices could include telephones, hand-held digital assistants, sensors and controls located within a few meters of each other.

ZigBee is one of the global standards of communication protocol formulated by the relevant task force under the IEEE 802.15 working group. The fourth in the series, WPAN Low Rate/ZigBee is the newest and provides specifications for devices that have low data rates, consume very low power and are thus characterized by long battery life. Other standards like Bluetooth and IrDA address high data rate applications such as voice, video and LAN communications.

The ZigBee Alliance[34] has been set up as "an association of companies working together to enable reliable, cost-effective, low-power, wirelessly networked, monitoring and control products based on an open global standard".

Once a manufacturer enrolls in this Alliance for a fee, he can have access to the standard and implement it in his products in the form of ZigBee chipsets that would be built into the end devices. Philips, Motorola, Intel, HP are all members of the Alliance . The goal is "to provide the consumer with ultimate flexibility, mobility, and ease of use by building wireless intelligence and capabilities into everyday devices.

ZigBee technology will be embedded in a wide range of products and applications across consumer, commercial, industrial and government markets

---

[34] "Zigbee Alliance." http://www.zigbee.org/. Accessed 18 Jan. 2018.

worldwide. For the first time, companies will have a standards-based wireless platform optimized for the unique needs of remote monitoring and control applications, including simplicity, reliability, low-cost and low-power".

The target networks encompass a wide range of devices with low data rates in the Industrial, Scientific and Medical (ISM) radio bands, with building-automation controls like intruder/fire alarms, thermostats and remote (wireless) switches, video/audio remote controls likely to be the most popular applications.

So far sensor and control devices have been marketed as proprietary items for the want of a standard. With acceptance and implementation of ZigBee, interoperability will be enabled in multi-purpose, self-organizing mesh networks

18. ZIGBEE ARCHITECTURE

Though WPAN implies a reach of only a few meters, 30 feet in the case of ZigBee, the network will have several layers, so designed as to enable intrapersonal communication within the network, connection to a network of higher level and ultimately an uplink to the Web.

The ZigBee Standard has evolved standardized sets of solutions, called 'layers'. These layers facilitate the features that make ZigBee very attractive: low cost, easy implementation, reliable data transfer, short-range operations, very low power consumption and adequate security features.

1. Network and Application Support Layer: The network layer permits growth of network sans high power transmitters. This layer can handle huge numbers of nodes. This level in the ZigBee architecture includes the ZigBee Device Object (ZDO), user-defined application profile(s) and the Application Support (APS) sub-layer.

The APS sub-layer's responsibilities include maintenance of tables that enable matching between two devices and communication among them, and also discovery, the aspect that identifies other devices that operate in the operating space of any device.

The responsibility of determining the nature of the device

81

(Coordinator / FFD or RFD) in the network, commencing and replying to binding requests and ensuring a secure relationship between devices rests with the ZDO (Zigbee Define Object). The user-defined application refers to the end device that conforms to the ZigBee Standard.

2. Physical (PHY) Layer: The IEEE 802.15.4 PHY physical layer accommodates high levels of integration by using direct sequence to permit simplicity in the analog circuitry and enable cheaper implementations.

3. Media access control (MAC) Layer: The IEEE 802.15.4 MAC media access control layer permits use of several topologies without introducing complexity and is meant to work with large numbers of devices.

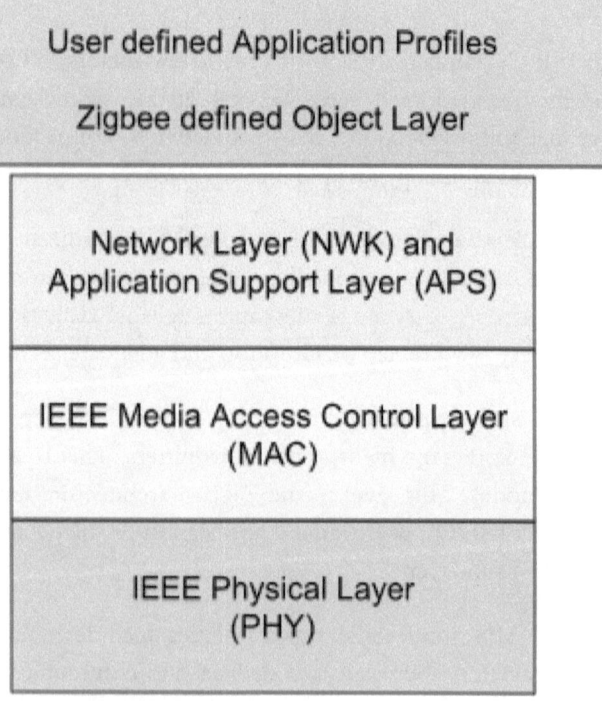

Figure 12: IEEE 802.15.4 / ZigBee Stack Architecture

19. ZIGBEE DEVICE TYPES

There are three different ZigBee device types that operate on these layers in any self-organizing application network.

These devices have 64-bit IEEE addresses, with option to enable shorter addresses to reduce packet size, and work in either of two addressing modes – star and peer-to-peer.

1. **The ZigBee Coordinator node:** There is one, and only one, ZigBee coordinator in each network to act as the router to other networks, and can be likened to the root of a (network) tree. It is designed to store information about the network.

2. **The Full Function Device (FFD)**: The FFD is an intermediary router transmitting data from other devices. It needs lesser memory than the ZigBee coordinator node, and entails lesser manufacturing costs. It can operate in all topologies and can act as a coordinator.

3. **The Reduced Function Device (RFD):** This device is just capable of talking in the network; it cannot relay data from other devices. Requiring even less memory, (no flash, very little ROM and RAM), an RFD will thus be cheaper than an FFD. This device talks only to a network coordinator and can be implemented very simply in star topology.

20. ZIGBEE CHARACTERISTICS

The focus of network applications under the IEEE 802.15.4 / ZigBee standard include the features of low power consumption, needed for only two major modes (Tx/Rx or Sleep), high density of nodes per network, low costs and simple implementation.

These features are enabled by the following characteristics[35] :

- 2.4GHz and 868/915 MHz dual PHY modes. This represents three license-free bands: 2.4-2.4835 GHz, 868-870 MHz and 902-928 MHz. The number of channels allotted to each frequency band is fixed at sixteen (numbered 11-26), one (numbered 0) and ten (numbered 1-10) respectively. The higher frequency band is applicable worldwide, and the lower band in the areas of North America, Europe, Australia and New Zealand.

- Low power consumption, with a battery life ranging from months to

[35] "Wireless Control That Simply Works - ZigBee Resource Guide." http://www.zigbeeresourceguide.com/images/ZigBee_RG_2008.pdf. Accessed 18 Jan. 2018.

years. Considering the number of devices with remotes in use at present, it is easy to see that more numbers of batteries need to be provisioned every so often, entailing regular (as well as timely), recurring expenditure. In the ZigBee standard, longer battery life is achievable by either of two means: continuous network connection and slow but sure battery drain, or intermittent connection and even slower battery drain.

- Maximum data rates allowed for each of these frequency bands are fixed as 250 kbps @2.4 GHz, 40 kbps @ 915 MHz, and 20 kbps @868 MHz.

- High throughput and low latency for low duty-cycle applications (<0.1%)

- Channel access using Carrier Sense Multiple Access with Collision Avoidance (CSMA - CA)

- Addressing space of up to 64 bit IEEE address devices, 65,535 networks

- 50m typical range

- Fully reliable "hand-shaked" data transfer protocol.

Different topologies as illustrated below: star, peer-to-peer, mesh

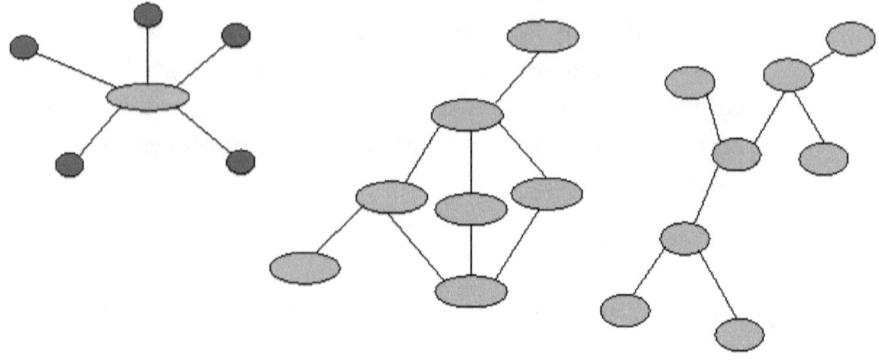

Figure 12: ZigBee Topologies

21. ZIGBEE TRAFFIC TYPES

ZigBee/IEEE 802.15.4 addresses three typical traffic types. IEEE 802.15.4 MAC can accommodate all the types.

1. **Data is periodic**: The application dictates the rate, and the sensor activates, checks for data and deactivates.

2. **Data is intermittent**:. The application, or other stimulus, determines the rate, as in the case of say smoke detectors. The device needs to connect to the network only when communication is necessitated. This type enables optimum saving on energy.

3. **Data is repetitive**, and the rate is fixed a priori. Depending on allotted time slots, called GTS (guaranteed time slot), devices operate for fixed durations.

ZigBee employs either of two modes, beacon or non-beacon to enable the to-and-fro data traffic. Beacon mode is used when the coordinator runs on batteries and thus offers maximum power savings, whereas the non-beacon mode finds favour when the coordinator is mains-powered.

In the beacon mode, a device watches out for the coordinator's beacon that gets transmitted at periodically, locks on and looks for messages addressed to it. If message transmission is complete, the coordinator dictates a schedule for the next beacon so that the device 'goes to sleep'; in fact, the coordinator itself switches to sleep mode.

While using the beacon mode, all the devices in a mesh network know when to communicate with each other. In this mode, necessarily, the timing circuits have to be quite accurate, or wake up sooner to be sure not to miss the beacon. This in turn means an increase in power consumption by the coordinator's receiver, entailing an optimal increase in costs.

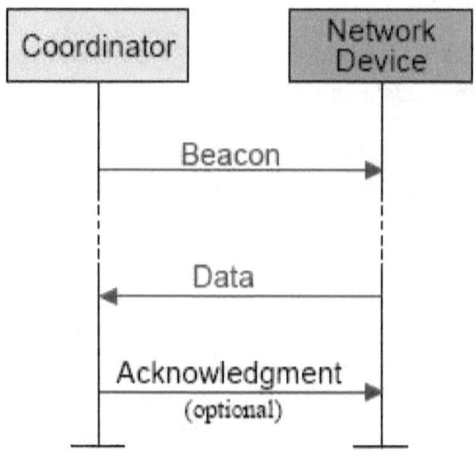

Figure 13: Beacon Network Communication

The non-beacon mode will be included in a system where devices are 'asleep' nearly always, as in smoke detectors and burglar alarms. The devices wake up and confirm their continued presence in the network at random intervals.

On detection of activity, the sensors 'spring to attention', as it were, and transmit to the ever-waiting coordinator's receiver (since it is mains-powered). However, there is the remotest of chances that a sensor finds the channel busy, in which case the receiver unfortunately would 'miss a call'.

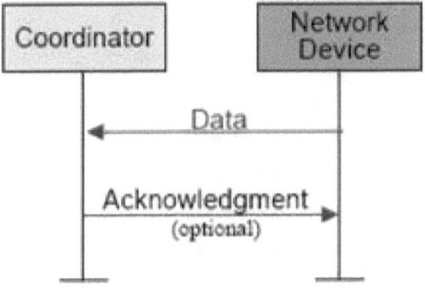

Figure 14: Non-Beacon Network Communication

gordon.colbach@cloudversity.com

22. ZIGBEE NETWORK MODEL

The functions of the Coordinator, which usually remains in the receptive mode, encompass network set-up, beacon transmission, node management, storage of node information and message routing between nodes.

The network node, however, is meant to save energy (and so 'sleeps' for long periods) and its functions include searching for network availability, data transfer, checks for pending data and queries for data from the coordinator.

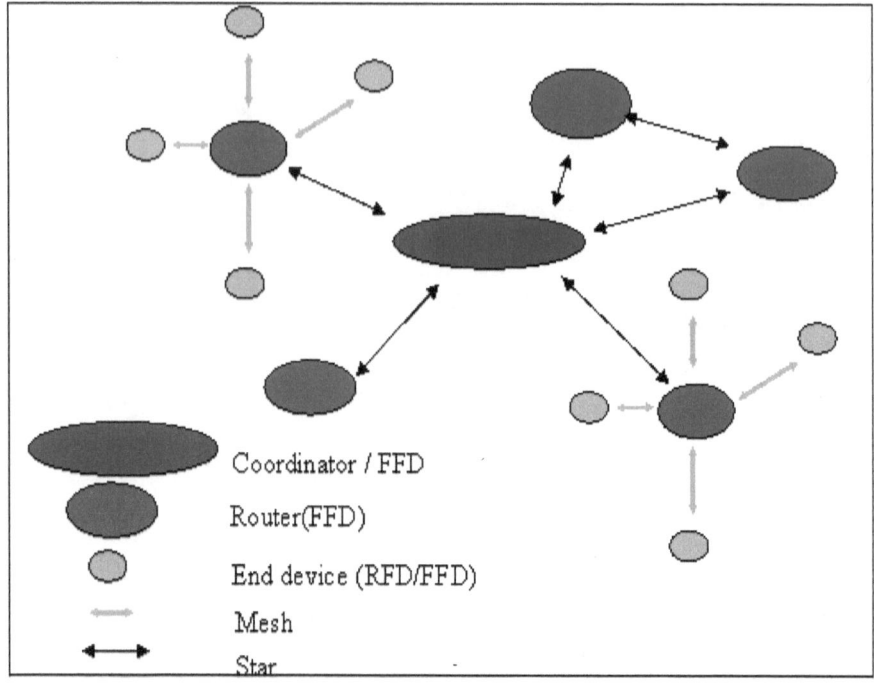

Figure 14: ZigBee Network Model

For the sake of simplicity without jeopardising robustness, this particular IEEE standard defines a quartet frame structure and a super-frame structure used optionally only by the coordinator.

The four frame structures are:

1. Beacon frame for transmission of beacons
2. Data frame for all data transfers
3. Acknowledgement frame for successful frame receipt confirmations
4. MAC command frame

These frame structures and the coordinator's super-frame structure play critical roles in security of data and integrity in transmission.

All protocol layers contribute headers and footers to the frame structure, such that the total overheads for each data packet range are from 15 octets (for short addresses) to 31 octets (for 64-bit addresses).

The coordinator lays down the format for the super-frame for sending beacons after every 15.38 ms or/and multiples thereof, up to 252s. This interval is determined a priori and the coordinator thus enables sixteen time slots of identical width between beacons so that channel access is contention-less.

Within each time slot, access is contention-based. Nonetheless, the coordinator provides as many as seven GTS (guaranteed time slots) for every beacon interval to ensure better quality.

gordon.colbach@cloudversity.com

23. ZIGBEE VS BLUETOOTH

The "Why ZigBee" question has always had an implied, but never quite worded follower phrase "…when there is Bluetooth".

The bandwidth of Bluetooth is 1 Mbps, ZigBee's is one-fourth of this value. The strength of Bluetooth lies in its ability to allow interoperability and replacement of cables, ZigBee's, of course, is low costs and long battery life.

In terms of protocol stack size, ZigBee's 32 KB is about one-third of the stack size necessary in other wireless technologies (for limited capability end devices, the stack size is as low as 4 KB).

Most important in any meaningful comparison are the diverse application areas of all the different wireless technologies. Bluetooth is meant for such target areas as wireless USB, handsets and headsets, whereas ZigBee is meant to cater to the sensors and remote controls market and other battery operated products.

In a gist, it may be said that they are neither complementary standards nor competitors, but just essential standards for different targeted applications. The earlier Bluetooth targets interfaces between PDA and other devices (mobile phone / printer etc) and cordless audio applications.

The IEEE 802.15.4–based ZigBee is designed for remote controls and sensors, which are very many in number, but need only small data packets and, mainly, extremely low power consumption for (long) life. Therefore they are naturally different in their approach to their respective application arenas.

24. ZIGBEE APPLICATIONS

The ZigBee Alliance[36] targets applications "across consumer, commercial, industrial and government markets worldwide".

Unwired applications are highly sought after in many networks that are characterized by numerous nodes consuming minimum power and enjoying long battery lives.

ZigBee technology is designed to best suit these applications, for the reason that it enables reduced costs of development, very fast market adoption, and rapid ROI.

Airbee Wireless Inc has tied up with Radiocrafts AS to deliver "out-of-the-box" ZigBee-ready solutions; the former supplying the software and the latter making the module platforms. With even light controls and thermostat producers joining the ZigBee Alliance, the list is growing healthily and includes big OEM names like HP, Philips, Motorola and Intel.

With ZigBee designed to enable two-way communications, not only will the consumer be able to monitor and keep track of domestic utilities

---

[36] "Zigbee Alliance." http://www.zigbee.org/. Accessed 18 Jan. 2018.

usage, but also feed it to a computer system for data analysis.

A recent analyst report issued by West Technology Research Solutions estimates that by the year 2008, "annual shipments for ZigBee chipsets into the home automation segment alone will exceed 339 million units," and will show up in "light switches, fire and smoke detectors, thermostats, appliances in the kitchen, video and audio remote controls, landscaping, and security systems."

Futurists are sure to hold ZigBee up and say, "See, I told you so". The ZigBee Alliance is nearly 200 strong and growing, with more OEM's signing up. This means that more and more products and even later, all devices and their controls will be based on this standard.

Since Wireless personal Area Networking applies not only to household devices, but also to individualised office automation applications, ZigBee is here to stay. It is more than likely the basis of future home-networking solutions.